The Baby Naming Journal

BY PAMELA REDMOND SATRAN
AND LINDA ROSENKRANTZ

CHRONICLE BOOKS

ILLUSTRATIONS: ELVIS SWIFT
DESIGN: SIMONE KANE
TYPESET IN MINION AND SERLIO

ISBN: 0-8118-2530-2
PRINTED IN HONG KONG

10 9 8 7 6 5 4 3 2 1

DISTRIBUTED IN CANADA BY
RAINCOAST BOOKS
8680 CAMBIE STREET
VANCOUVER, B.C. V6P 6M9

CHRONICLE BOOKS
85 SECOND STREET
SAN FRANCISCO, CA 94105
WWW.CHRONICLEBOOKS.COM

Dedicated to

_____

With love from

_____

_____

Date

Table of Contents

Acknowledgments

Our thanks to Debra Lande, Jodi Davis,
Christina Henry, Karen Shapiro, and Jane Sandor.

introduction

A name is the first and most enduring gift you bestow on your child. Forever after, a name stands as a symbol of your hopes and dreams, your child's history and future. Choosing a name that fulfills this promise is a significant responsibility, and also one that can bring you enormous pleasure in the months leading up to your baby's arrival.

This journal is designed to guide you through the work and the fun of finding the perfect name for your child. It will give you and your spouse a way to find names you both love, as well as help you reconcile your differing opinions. It will show you how to delve into your family's past for naming inspiration, as well as how to deal with family pressures on name choices. **The Baby Naming Journal** *will help you search for meaningful, creative names and navigate all your options to arrive at the one that's ideal for you and your child.*

Baby naming has become a more involved—and involving—activity than ever before. Parents are looking far beyond the obvious name choices to names that have lain dormant for years, that have only been used in other countries and cultures, that until now have not even been used as first names. They're hunting for ideas in a range of books and on an ever-growing number of Web sites; they're combing family trees, world atlases, phone books, and even dictionaries in search of unusual and interesting names.

That makes this baby naming journal even more essential as a place where you can sift through and record the myriad name ideas you encounter in your research and conversations. At last, something more permanent, more useful than scribbled-on scraps of paper! Not only can this journal help you keep track of the names you find, it can give you a way to think about those names and record the ideas and feelings that lead you to your ultimate choice.

You can dip in and out of this journal, finding the sections that seem most relevant to your own search and setting down your ideas in those places. Or you can go through the process from beginning to end, starting with the personal—working through name ideas with spouse, family, and friends, as well as considering your hopes and dreams for your child—then progressing through the universal range of name possibilities.

The record you keep on your journey toward your child's name becomes the perfect keepsake, giving your child an invaluable insight into all the thoughts and emotions that went into choosing his or her name. It's a personal heirloom your child and your family will treasure for generations.

mother & father

YOU AGREE ON HOW MUCH YOU'LL LOVE
YOUR NEW BABY. BUT WILL YOU EVER AGREE
ON A NAME? HERE, YOU'LL FIND A PLACE TO
RECORD NAMES YOU EACH LIKE, AS WELL AS
SEVERAL SUGGESTIONS ON HOW TO FIND A
NAME YOU'LL BOTH ADORE.

MOM'S FAVORITE NAMES

What names do you love most? List them here (adding new favorites as you move through the baby naming process) and see how your partner feels about your top choices.

MOM'S FAVORITES   DAD'S COMMENTS

_____   _____

_____   _____

_____   _____

_____   _____

_____   _____

_____   _____

_____   _____

_____   _____

_____   _____

_____   _____

_____   _____

_____   _____

_____   _____

_____   _____

_____   _____

DAD'S FAVORITE NAMES

Now, the tables turn. Here's where Dad notes his favorite names and Mom provides her comments.

DAD'S FAVORITES

MOM'S COMMENTS

Mom's "No" List

It can be just as useful to list the names you can't stand as the ones you love. Agree up front: Names on each partner's "No" list will be taken out of the running.

_____   _____

_____   _____

_____   _____

_____   _____

_____   _____

_____   _____

_____   _____

_____   _____

_____   _____

_____   _____

_____   _____

_____   _____

_____   _____

Dad's "No" List

Dad's turn to construct his list of "Absolutely nots."

THE NAMES DAD ABSOLUTELY, POSITIVELY,
WON'T CONSIDER FOR THE BABY:

_____   _____

_____   _____

_____   _____

_____   _____

_____   _____

_____   _____

_____   _____

_____   _____

_____   _____

_____   _____

_____   _____

_____   _____

_____   _____

_____   _____

Two Thumbs Up

Names you both love are apt to constantly shift over the weeks and months you search for the perfect name. Use this page to keep track of th[e] front-runners.

Seal *of* APPROVAL

YOU SAY MAKAYLA, I SAY MAKENNA

The baby was a week overdue, and the anxious parents were sitting in a restaurant, scribbling on the paper tablecloth. "Eliza," wrote the mom-to-be. But Dad scratched it off. "Too weird," he proclaimed, replacing it with "Rachel."

"Too ordinary," said Mom. After one or the other of them rejected every girls' name from Molly to Malloy, the about-to-be-a-mother sighed, "It better be a boy."

Why do so many couples have so many problems finding a name both partners love? Partly because you're still individuals, with individual tastes, predilections, and experiences. And usually, one of you is a man and the other a woman; studies show that women tend to be more adventurous and modern in their take on names, while men tend to be more traditional.

A Few Techniques for Reaching an Accord in the Name Wars

* *Talk about the child before you discuss the name.* What sort of child do you each hope for? A delicate little angel or the soccer team's high scorer? A real individual or someone who'll carry on the family traditions? These discussions can lead you to a name that reflects your hopes and dreams—they can also help you agree on how to raise your child.

* *Leave the past behind.* Forget the names of all past loves, ex-friends, childhood tormentors, and cigar-chomping great-uncles.

* *Respect individual differences.* Try to find a name you both like, rather than seizing control of the name from your partner. If you can't agree, then one of you might choose the first name and the other the middle name, alternating with the next child. Or one of you might give the baby a first name, the other a surname.

family & friends

For better or worse, family and friends are intricate parts of the baby naming process. Here's where you can record other people's name ideas, if only for your child's future amusement. But family can also be an important source of name inspiration. In this section you can also search for family names that might be right for your child.

How About Junior?

It's worked for Tom Cruise and Clint Eastwood and Johnny Depp and Magic Johnson—all of them Juniors—and it could work for your son, too, especially if it's a long-standing tradition in your family to name a son after his father in order to preserve a specific name intact. Sharing a name forges a strong father-son bond and can even be seen as a vote of confidence that the boy will live up to his father's name.

But be aware that the practice can lead to certain confusions—and even some negative side effects. If father and son are identically named Joseph Francis Farley and both are called Joe, embarrassing situations can result from inevitably misdirected mail and phone calls. If they are "Big Joe" and "Little Joe" or "Joe" and "Joey" for life, the son may feel somewhat demeaned, and if the child is known as Junior (or Sonny or Buddy), he might grow up feeling like a lesser, junior citizen.

One way around this problem is to give the child a different middle name, say Joseph Austin, and call him Austin, thereby still honoring his father but successfully circumventing the various Junior obstacles. And when he's an important grown-up executive, he can always sign himself J. Austin Farley.

NAMESAKES

Did Great-great-uncle Arthur ride in the cavalry in the Civil War? Did Grandmother Bridget make her way to America all alone at age sixteen? These family stories can make the names come alive for your little name-sake. Here, record the stories connected to the names you're considering. If you have photographs, include them here.

_____

_____

_____

_____

_____

_____

_____

_____

_____

_____

_____

_____

_____

_____

_____

(PHOTOS HERE)

OUTSIDE INFLUENCES

*When it comes to naming the baby, everybody's got an opinion. Write
down who thinks you should choose which name, and why.*

WHO	THE NAME	WHY

FAMILY PRESSURE

They're trying to be helpful. They're only thinking of the family and of the baby's best interests. And they're driving you crazy.

You might be able to laugh off the fifteen variations on Margaret suggested by your mother-in-law, whose name just happens to be . . . Margaret. But name pressure often gets more intense and more difficult to deflect. Not only can families bombard you with their ideas on what you should name the baby, they can be hyper-critical of your own choices.

But your child's name is your decision.

HOW TO GET THE FAMILY OFF YOUR NAMING CASE:

* ***Make it a joke.*** *When they ask what you're naming the baby, say, "Harold Aloysius." Or "Ethel Mildred Summer Winter." In other words, stun them speechless.*

* ***Invent a decoy name.*** *Deflect all naming suggestions by saying you're sorry, but your mind is made up, you're naming the baby Colin John. Listen calmly to all critiques of Colin John. You don't care, because you know the birth certificate's going to read Christopher James.*

* ***Consider their suggestions.*** *Maybe Mom really has found a great family name, or Dad has a good reason you shouldn't name the baby after Grandma Rose. Hear them out. Turn it into a game. But don't let them make the decision.*

* ***Lay down the law.*** *If you've tried laughing, ignoring, and listening, and you're still feeling unbearable pressure, it's time to tell the relatives in no uncertain terms that this is your baby and you get to name him, and that's the last you want to hear about it.* **Ever.**

naming a daughter

IN THE FACE OF CHANGING GENDER IMAGES AND IDEALS, NAMING A GIRL HAS BECOME SIGNIFICANTLY MORE COMPLICATED. OF COURSE, MOST GIRLS' NAMES ARE STILL CONVENTIONALLY FEMALE—BUT DO YOU PREFER A NAME WITH A MORE SERIOUS GROWN-UP IMAGE, SUCH AS ELIZABETH OR CHARLOTTE, OR DO YOU LIKE GIRLISH NAMES SUCH AS HALLIE OR ANNIE? DOES AN ULTRAFEMININE NAME SUCH AS GABRIELLA OR ALLEGRA REPRESENT A RETROGRADE IDEA OF FEMININITY OR A POSTMODERN ONE?

AND THEN THERE IS THE WHOLE NEW RAFT OF GIRLS' NAMES THAT BREAK FEMALE STEREOTYPES. YOU MIGHT CHOOSE ONE OF THE NEW ANDROGYNOUS NAMES FOR YOUR BABY GIRL: A SURNAME-NAME LIKE TAYLOR, A PLACE NAME LIKE PARIS, A WORD OR NATURE NAME SUCH AS JUNIPER. OR BREAK ALL THE RULES AND GO FOR A GENUINE BOY'S NAME; SUCH FAVORITES AS RYAN, JEREMY, OR ZACHARY SOUND NEW WHEN USED FOR GIRLS.

What are your hopes and dreams for your daughter as a girl and as a woman? What sort of image do you hold for the person you want your child to become: smart, creative, energetic, beautiful? List some of your ideas and the names that might fit them.

FATHER'S IDEAS

How do you envision your little girl? Do you see her as an athlete or an artist, a great beauty, a world leader, or all of the above? Write down a few of your hopes and dreams for your daughter's future, and the names that fit these images.

WHEN I WAS A LITTLE GIRL...

Growing up, how did you feel about your own name? What did you wish you had been named? What were the names you imagined someday giving your own little girls? And how do you want your daughter to feel about the name you choose for her?

FROM MARY TO MADISON

Throughout most of this country's history, Mary reigned as the queen of girls' names. But in 1948, the much more modern-sounding Linda knocked Mary out of first place, and baby naming was never the same again. Linda was joined by other contemporary names like Karen and Sharon, all reflecting a shiny new and optimistic post-war suburban culture.

Baby names, particularly for girls, say a lot about society in general. By 1970, Jennifer topped the girls' popularity list. Other trendy names of the late sixties and seventies—Jessie and Jamie, Kelly and Kim—evidenced the break with sexual stereotypes ushered in by the feminist movement. In the early eighties, such ambisexual names as Ashley, Brittany, Courtney, and Lindsay climbed up the popularity list.

Now, the favorite names for girls have taken a more serious turn. Biblical names like Sarah, Rachel, Hannah, and Abigail have become increasingly popular as have other solid, traditional names from the past—Emily, Emma, Elizabeth, Katherine. The taste for androgynous names continues with even-more-masculine-sounding choices: Taylor, Madison, Jordan, Morgan.

And what ever happened to Mary? According to recent Social Security figures, it has fallen to Number 58—sandwiched between Carly and Cheyenne.

naming a son

Today's shifting conceptions of gender identity make naming a son a difficult enterprise. With more and more parents choosing formerly masculine names for their daughters, it's becoming increasingly difficult to find boys' names that are distinctly male. The big question: Do you care—and will your son care—if he shares a name with a female classmate (or two or three)?

You may want to sidestep gender confusion by choosing one of the more traditional male names: John, Robert, William, etc. If that name pool is too narrow for you and you want a more creative (but still clearly masculine) choice, you might consider a non-English name—a Latin favorite such as Carlo, for example, or an Irish name like Liam or Cormac. Note: When naming sons, most parents—and especially fathers—still favor more traditional and family-connected names than they do when choosing names for their daughters.

MOTHER'S IDEAS

Do you want a traditional male image for your son or a more modern one? Record some of your hopes and dreams, and think of names that might fulfill them.

FATHER'S IDEAS

How do you see your son as a little boy and as a man? What are your hopes and dreams for the person he'll become, and how do your name choices fit those?

_____

_____

_____

_____

_____

_____

_____

_____

_____

_____

_____

_____

_____

_____

_____

_____

Growing up, how did you feel about your own name? Are there names you wished you had instead of your own? And how do you hope your son will feel about the name you choose for him?

ARE THERE ANY BOYS' NAMES LEFT?

When it comes to names, how can you tell the men from the boys...from the girls? The following lists suggest traditional male names with all-boy appeal; some new choices for boys; and androgynous names that have shifted far—perhaps too far—into female territory.

TRADITIONAL BOYS

Andrew	*Charles*
Daniel	*Edward*
Henry	*James*
Joseph	*Peter*
Thomas	*William*

NEW BOYS

Aidan	*Brennan*
Emmett	*Hunter*
Jonah	*Logan*
Owen	*Quentin*
Riley	*Sawyer*

TOO GIRLISH?

Ashley	*Cheyenne*
Courtney	*Devon*
Kelsey	*Mackenzie*
Morgan	*Sierra*
Sydney	*Taylor*

styles & trends

MANY OF THE MOST IMPORTANT NAME TRENDS THESE DAYS RELATE TO PERSONAL STYLE: FINDING A NAME THAT REFLECTS YOUR TASTES, YOUR EXPERIENCES, YOUR BACKGROUND, YOUR FAMILY. THERE ARE OLD-FASHIONED NAMES PLUCKED FROM THE FAMILY TREE, SURNAME-NAMES THAT REVIVE AN OTHERWISE-LOST PIECE OF FAMILY HISTORY, CULTURALLY EVOCATIVE NAMES THAT TAP INTO YOUR ROOTS, PLACE NAMES AND WORD NAMES SYMBOLIC OF YOUR LIFE AND SOUL.

WHAT'S YOUR STYLE?

What's your personal style, and how does it relate to names? Below are descriptions of the main naming styles and lists of individual names that fit into them. Record your feelings about each category to decipher which one most closely resembles you. Knowing your overall style preferences can help you hunt for other names that may be right for your child. The names included on these lists are just examples and are by no means definitive; you can find literally hundreds more names to suit each style.

TRADITIONAL/CLASSIC

GIRLS	BOYS
Anne	Andrew
Caroline	Christopher
Charlotte	Daniel
Claire	Edward
Eleanor	James
Elizabeth	John
Jane	Joseph
Julia	Peter
Katherine	Thomas
Margaret	William

___ WE LOVE THIS STYLE
___ WE MIGHT CONSIDER IT
___ IT'S REALLY NOT US

Gently Old-Fashioned

GIRLS	BOYS
Alice	*Charles*
Amelia	*Emmett*
Beatrice	*Frederick*
Flora	*George*
Isabel	*Harry*
Louisa	*Henry*
Lucy	*Hugh*
Maude	*Jasper*
Rose	*Julian*
Sophia	*Philip*

___ WE LOVE THIS STYLE
___ WE MIGHT CONSIDER
___ IT'S REALLY NOT US

Popular

GIRLS	BOYS
Alexis	*Austin*
Alyssa	*Brandon*
Ashley	*Cameron*
Brianna	*Christian*
Haley	*Dylan*
Kaitlyn	*Jordan*
Madison	*Joshua*
Makayla	*Justin*
Savannah	*Kyle*
Taylor	*Tyler*

___ WE LOVE THIS STYLE
___ WE MIGHT CONSIDER
___ IT'S REALLY NOT US

CREATIVE/ORIGINAL

GIRLS	BOYS
Alcott	Abraham
Cairo	Amos
Clementine	Dexter
Dominick	Fielder
Juniper	Hugo
Keturah	Isaiah
Luna	Mercury
Octavia	Obadiah
Pansy	Phineas
Violet	Sullivan

___ WE LOVE THIS STYLE
___ WE MIGHT CONSIDER IT
___ IT'S REALLY NOT US

CULTURALLY DIVERSE

GIRLS	BOYS
Adriana	Amadeo
Bronwen	Bjorn
Chiara	Emilio
Deirdre	Gunter
Elodie	Leonardo
Ingrid	Luc
Maeve	Malcolm
Nicola	Raoul
Saskia	Seamus
Yasmin	Willem

___ WE LOVE THIS STYLE
___ WE MIGHT CONSIDER IT
___ IT'S REALLY NOT US

Friendly

Girls	Boys
Annie	*Ben*
Billie	*Charlie*
Daisy	*Gus*
Gracie	*Jack*
Josie	*Jake*
Molly	*Joe*
Nellie	*Max*
Sadie	*Nat*
Sophie	*Ned*
Tillie	*Sam*

___We love this style
___We might consider i
___It's really not us

MICHAEL MANIA

Michael has been the number-one boy's name for half a century, with several tens of thousands of Michaels born in the United States each year. Why the name's overwhelming popularity? Because it can be everything to everybody. The Greek form of an ancient Hebrew name meaning "Who is like the Lord," Michael is used by Christians, Jews, and Muslims alike; by parents looking for a traditional male name; as well as by those interested in a name that's modern and melodic. Michael is the name of an archangel, as well as the patron saint of soldiers, bankers, radiologists, and policemen. Other famous Michaels include Jordan, Jackson, Douglas, and J. Fox, as well as nine Byzantine emperors, five Romanian kings, and a Tsar of Russia. Foreign variations include Michel (French), Miguel (Spanish), and Mikhail (Russian); common nicknames are Mike, Mickey, and Mick.

What's Everyone Else Doing?

What are the other babies in your life being named? What are the names of your child's future cousins and playmates, his classmates and contemporaries? Here, keep track of all the new names you hear.

FAMILY BABIES' NAMES

FRIENDS' BABIES' NAMES

CELEBRITIES' BABIES' NAMES

BABY NAMES FOUND ONLINE

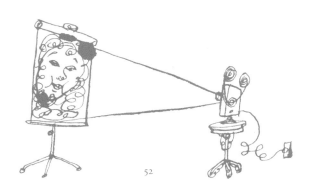

52

NAMES FROM NEWSPAPER BIRTH ANNOUNCEMENTS

NAME POPULARITY LISTS

Out of Oblivion

You'd like your child to stand out by virtue of his or her intriguing name—does that mean you have to invent a new name or a "creative" spelling? Not necessarily. You can also look back to names that have been napping for a couple of generations and are now ready to wake up and face the world. They may sound nearly new, but these names carry a true sense of history, tradition, meaning, and vintage charm. Here are just a few examples:

GIRLS	BOYS
Ada	*Artemas*
Augusta	*Barnabas*
Christabel	*Benedict*
Cornelia	*Clement*
Cressida	*Conrad*
Emmeline	*Ezekiel*
Evangeline	*Jarvis*
Genevieve	*Lucius*
Theodora	*Quincy*
Viola	*Thaddeus*

NAMES OF THE FUTURE

What names do you like that are on the cutting edge of fashion? Here's the place to record intriguing names and ideas that might prove inspirational to you.

unusual names

LET'S SAY YOU DON'T WANT YOUR CHILD TO
BE ONE OF SEVERAL KIDS WITH THE SAME
NAME IN HER CLASS—SWIMMING IN A
CROWDED SEA OF SARAHS OR SAMANTHAS—
YOU WANT HER TO HAVE A NAME THAT IS
DISTINCTIVE, PERHAPS EVEN UNIQUE.
HERE IS AN OPPORTUNITY FOR YOU TO
EXPERIMENT WITH THE ALMOST ENDLESS
VARIETY OF CREATIVE NAME POSSIBILITIES.

PLACE NAMES

Many parents now find inspiration not in name books but in atlases, or in recalling places that hold personal significance. One celebrity couple, for example, used the name of their honeymoon hotel in New York, the Carlyle, as the middle name for not one but two of their daughters. Think about the geography of your relationship, romantic places you've enjoyed together, places with family history, or places with names whose resonance you simply like. One of these place names might be perfect for your child.

ANCESTRAL COUNTRIES, CITIES, AND TOWNS

PLACES WHERE YOU'VE LIVED OR GONE TO SCHOOL

WHERE YOU MET

WHERE YOU GOT MARRIED

YOUR HONEYMOON SPOT

FAVORITE TRAVELS

OTHER ATTRACTIVE PLACE NAMES

If Madonna Can Do It...

Celebrities, almost by definition, possess a certain flamboyance, and this is often as evident in their children's names as in their on- and off-screen personas. Movie, television, music, and sports stars have been on the forefront of many naming trends such as selecting geographic names for their sons and daughters, using boys' names for girls, or importing unusual foreign names. Some have moved beyond these adventurous categories to venture into even more exotic territory, as exemplified by:

Girls

Aquinnah — *Tracy Pollan and Michael J. Fox*
Deni Montana — *Woody Harrelson*
Destry Allyn — *Kate Capshaw and Steven Spielberg*
Ireland Eliesse — *Kim Basinger and Alec Baldwin*
Lourdes Maria — *Madonna*
Sailor Lee — *Christie Brinkley*
Satchel Lewis — *Spike Lee*
Scout Larue — *Demi Moore and Bruce Willis*
Sistine Rose — *Jennifer Flavin and Sylvester Stallone*
Sosie Ruth — *Kyra Sedgwick and Kevin Bacon*

BOYS

ARPAD FLYNN — *Elle Macpherson*
BRAISON CHANCE — *Billy Ray Cyrus*
BRAWLEY KING — *Nick Nolte*
BUCK — *Roseanne*
GULLIVER FLYNN — *Gary Oldman*
HOPPER JACK — *Robin Wright and Sean Penn*
JETT — *Kelly Preston and John Travolta*
REBOP — *Todd Rundgren*
SPECK WILDHORSE — *John Mellencamp*
ZION — *Lauryn Hill and Rohan Marley*

WORD NAMES

A fisherman names his son Pike. A gardener's daughter is called Lilac. I
several cultures, children may be named for the season, month, holiday, o
time of birth: Autumn, May, Noel, Afternoon. Virtue names, dating from the
Puritans, are fair game, too: Honor, Patience. The Puritans often extende
this practice by using significant words as names—Remember, Experience—
while modern parents are popularizing names such as Heaven and Destiny
Colors—Amber, Gray—and gems—Ruby, Pearl—are also possibilities.

This is a place for you to list all the words you might consider as names.

FLOWERS/PLANTS

ANIMALS

COLORS

GEMS

VIRTUES

SEASONS/HOLIDAYS/MONTHS

OTHER WORD NAMES

VARIATIONS

Changing the form of a classic name—say from Valerie to Valeria, from Rachel to Raquel, Alexander to Zan—can be another route to a more creative name. Here's where you can play with those possibilities. But beware of making the changes so extreme that the child's name becomes confusing to everyone. . . including her.

ORIGINAL NAME	POSSIBLE VARIATIONS

Another road leading towards an unusual name is to vary the spelling of the name. Many celebrities have created unique identities for themselves in this way, from Diahann Carroll and Dyan Cannon, to Khrystyne Haye and Camryn Manheim. Certainly, a distinctive spelling can make an old name feel newer (Carly to Karleigh, Jason to Jaysen), but your child may face a few difficulties as she grows older. She will have to constantly correct people who aren't aware that Sierra can also be spelled Ceara and who might assume that her parents had been poor players in the phonics game. Before you decide to change the spelling of a name like Ann to Ahn, you might consider an authentic foreign variant, such as Anika or Anya, or a related name with a similar sound, say, Annabel or Antonia.

UNIQUE NAMES

This page is a worksheet for creating a name that is really special, one that no other child will have. You can try, for instance, combining your name with your husband's or those of the baby's two grandmothers or grandfathers; one couple came up with Lorelia, honoring Grandmas Lorraine and Delia. Or you can go further afield and experiment with appealing sounds, combining them to form a new and unique name.

*used to be very easy to judge whether a name was common or rare:
ary was common, Mariah was not. But these days, when Jayla is far more
opular than Jane, the line has blurred— it's tricky figuring out which
ames are widely used and which can still be considered unusual. The
llowing names, for example, may sound out-of-the-ordinary, but all of
em were used for at least 500 babies in the past year—and some of them
r thousands.*

ɪʀʟs	Bᴏʏs
ᴏndra	Ashton
shlyn	Braden
ubrey	Braxton
eja	Chance
elaney	Gage
enesis	Jace
eaven	Jaylen
da	Keaton
ylee	Kyler
esena	Trevon

the meaning of names

LIKE MANY OTHER PARENTS TODAY, YOU PROBABLY ARE SEARCHING FOR A NAME THAT HAS MEANING, WHETHER IT BE THE PERSONAL MEANING OF A FAMILY OR PLACE NAME, THE MEANING EMBODIED IN A CULTURALLY OR RELIGIOUSLY SIGNIFICANT NAME, OR THE LITERAL MEANING THAT REFLECTS A NAME'S ROOTS AND DERIVATION.

MOTHER'S ROOTS

*Is your background Scottish? Chinese? African-American? Armenian?
List possibilities from the baby's maternal ethnic heritage here, using family trees as well as reference books.*

FATHER'S ROOTS

Do the same thing here for Dad's cultural background.

CROSS-CULTURAL CHOICES

Many names span several different ethnic backgrounds, and exist, with slight variations, in different languages. Alejandro is Spanish, for example, while Alexei is Russian and Alistair is Scottish—all of them translations of the mega-popular Alexander. You might consider translating a name that you like into another language to arrive at a more distinctive version. If you want to honor a family member—say, your mother-in-law Barbara—but find that name somewhat dated, you could transform it into the livelier Swedish Barbro. Or you could change the even more untimely Bertha into the pretty French Bertille.

If you and your partner come from diverse ethnic cultures, you might seek out a name that exists in both. Ken and Alisa, for example, are names in both Japanese and English. You could also take a name reflecting Mom's ethnicity and use it as a middle name. Don't be afraid to mix styles—you might arrive at a great combination like Blanchette O'Brien or Emilio Jones.

RELIGIOUS BACKGROUND

Different religions have distinctive naming customs and considerations, from using (or not using) living relatives' names, to giving the child the name of an important religious figure. Investigate the customs of your religion, note them here, and list the names that satisfy them.

Naming Ceremonies and Rituals

The power of names is evident in naming ceremonies both modern and ancient. At the root of many naming ceremonies—from the baptisms and bris ceremonies familiar to present-day Americans to elaborate Native American naming rituals—is the desire to ward off evil spirits and marshal protective spiritual forces. Ashkenazi Jews traditionally believe that each name contains the very essence of life. For that reason, they don't give children a living relative's name, for fear of shortening the older person's lifespan.

In some cases, ritual provides a way for the child to choose his own name. The tradition among the Lango tribe in Africa, for example, is for a name to be offered to the baby along with the mother's breast. If the baby refuses to drink, other names are presented until the child responds. Maori babies are dressed in feathers and held by a priest who recites a litany of ancestral names. When the baby sneezes or cries, he has announced to the family his true name.

Heroes

Naming your child in honor of one of your personal heroes—from Georgie (O'Keeffe) to (Emily) Brontë to Shaquille (O'Neal), is another excellent way to invest a name with meaning. On this page, list the heroes whose names, first or last, might prove inspirational to you.

_____   _____

_____   _____

_____   _____

_____   _____

_____   _____

_____   _____

_____   _____

_____   _____

_____   _____

_____   _____

_____   _____

_____   _____

_____   _____

_____   _____

CHARACTERS

On this page, list the names of characters from books, movies, television, or songs, which might spark an idea for your child's name.

FAVORITE LITERARY CHARACTERS

CHARACTERS IN MOVIES

TELEVISION CHARACTERS

NAMES FROM SONGS

Dickens' Heroes

While some of us might consider naming our children after characters from the novels of Charles Dickens—Arabella in **The Pickwick Papers**, *Barnaby in* **Barnaby Rudge**, *or Quebec in* **Bleak House**—*Dickens himself named his seven sons after other literary lights he admired:*

Alfred Tennyson Dickens
Francis Jeffrey Dickens
Henry Fielding Dickens
Sydney Smith Haldimand Dickens
Walter Landor Dickens
Edward Bulwer Lytton Dickens
Charles Culliford Boz Dickens
(This last one after himself).

THE MEANING OF MAX

What do your favorite names mean? Look up the literal meanings of names you are considering and write them down here.

middle names

AFTER SETTLING ON YOUR FIRST NAME
FRONT-RUNNERS, IT'S TIME TO TURN YOUR
ATTENTION TO THE RIDDLE OF THE MIDDLE:
FINDING A NAME THAT MAKES A PERFECT
SANDWICH WHEN COMBINED WITH THE
FIRST AND LAST NAMES.

MIDDLE NAME IDEAS

Middle names have taken on a new and heightened importance, and you may be giving almost as much thought to the name in this position as to the first name. No longer are girls automatically assigned one of the traditional designated middle names—Ann, Lynn, Lee, Sue, Beth, or Marie. Modern parents see the middle name as an opportunity for creativity and adventurousness, as a way to honor an esteemed relative, friend or hero. Some directions you might explore:

* Follow the tradition of using a single-syllable name, but instead of the old standards, try something crisper (Brooke, Paige, Drew) or softer (Rose, Claire, Bryn).

* Consider the stylish possibility of using a boy's name for your daughter's middle name, a hot trend with celebrities. Diane Keaton's daughter, for example, is Dexter Dean (a unisex double-header), Kate Capshaw and Steven Spielberg have both a Destry Allyn and a Mikaela George, Annette Bening and Warren Beatty an Isabel Ira Ashley, Meredith Viera a Lily Max, and Demi Moore and Bruce Willis a Rumer Glenn. Some other boy names with middle-name potential for girls: Boyd, Lloyd, Claude, Cole, Craig, James, Jay, Kent, Lorne, Paul, Sean, Scott, Seth, Zane.

* *Observe the custom of using the mother's maiden name as the child's middle name, or take the practice a step further and consider other ancestral surnames, reviving grandma's maiden name for the next generation, for example.*

* *If one of you really loved a first name that the other vetoed, perhaps you could compromise by putting it in the middle spot.*

* *If you lean towards a traditional first name, you might want to be more adventurous here and choose a place name (Dublin or Ireland), a word name (True or Teal), a non-English name, a surname (from your family or someone else's), or the name of a literary character or personal hero.*

* *Use this spot to honor a relative whose name seems somewhat out-of-step with today's taste—say, Matilda or Edmund. Or if the name is too unpalatable, change it slightly, transforming Mildred to Millicent or Bertha to Belle.*

MIDDLE NAME POSSIBILITIES

Use this space to list potential middle names.

Try your middle name possibilities out between your favorite first names and your last name, saying each out loud to test its rhythm and compatibility.

nicknames

MOST PARENTS HAVE STRONG FEELINGS ONE WAY OR THE OTHER ABOUT NICKNAMES. ONE OF TODAY'S DOMINANT TRENDS IS TO CALL A CHILD SOLELY BY HIS PROPER NAME, SAY KATHERINE OR EDWARD. OTHER PARENTS CHOOSE A NAME WITH A SPECIFIC NICKNAME IN MIND—KATE OR NED, FOR INSTANCE—BUT ARE HORRIFIED BY THE IDEA THAT THEIR CHILD MIGHT BE CALLED KATHY OR EDDIE. THE PROBLEM WITH NICKNAMES IS THAT ONCE YOUR CHILD GOES TO SCHOOL, YOU HAVE NO CONTROL OVER THEM. THE BEST ADVICE: ANTICIPATE THE POSSIBILITIES, AND IF YOU REALLY DISLIKE NICKNAMES, CHOOSE A NAME THAT DOESN'T HAVE ANY.

The Nickname Anticipator

Consider the nicknames most commonly used for your front-running possibilities and evaluate whether they change how you feel about the name.

Name

Possible Nickname

Can We Live with It?

Do We Love It?

THE FIRST JAMIE

Nicknames sprang to life out of necessity in medieval England, when there were so few Christian names to go around that more than half the female population was named Mary, Anne, or Elizabeth. Because of this limited supply, it wasn't unusual for two children in a family to share a name. But since you couldn't call both of them Mary, one might become Molly, the other Polly—one Richard could be Dick, the other Hitch (rhyming was a favorite route to new nicknames). It wasn't until several centuries later that many of these pet forms—such as Sally, Betsy, Daisy, Peggy, and Nancy—were considered legitimate names, contributing greatly to the growing stock of options for English-speaking parents.

You might find some of the forgotten nicknames of the past well worth looking into, so that if you don't want your Caroline to be called Carrie, you could consider Caro. Or Maisie for Margaret. And instead of the usual Chris for Christopher, you might resurrect the almost-forgotten Kit, Kip, or Christy.

last names

MANY PARENTS NO LONGER TAKE IT FOR
GRANTED THAT THE BABY WILL SHARE ITS
FATHER'S LAST NAME. SURE, MOST PARENTS
STILL DO IT THE TRADITIONAL WAY, WITH
THE CHILDREN USING THEIR FATHER'S SUR-
NAME EVEN WHEN THE MOM KEEPS HER OWN
NAME: JACK PHILLIPS AND JILL MASON, FOR
INSTANCE, BECOME THE PARENTS OF
SABRINA PHILLIPS. BUT OTHER OPTIONS
THAT HAVE EMERGED INCLUDE: HYPHENAT-
ING THE PARENTAL SURNAMES (SABRINA
PHILLIPS-MASON); USING THE MOTHER'S
LAST NAME FOR DAUGHTERS, THE FATHER'S
FOR SONS (SABRINA MASON AND ZACHARY
PHILLIPS); AND HAVING MOM AND DAD
BOTH RETAIN THEIR BIRTH SURNAMES
WHILE COMBINING SYLLABLES FROM EACH
TO CREATE A NEW LAST NAME FOR THEIR
BABY (SABRINA PHILSON). SOME COUPLES
INVENT AN ENTIRELY NEW SURNAME FOR
THE WHOLE FAMILY TO SHARE (JACK, JILL,
SABRINA AND ZACHARY HEMINGWAY).

ere's where you can try out variations on the baby's last name, both on eir own and coupled with first and middle names you're considering.

Why We Chose This Last Name

Enter here your last name decision with an explanation of what led you to this choice.

LAST NAME

WHY WE CHOSE THIS LAST NAME

test drive

You've considered all the options, discussed, compared, contemplated, and eliminated. You're down to the final choices and last-minute considerations.

THE FINALISTS

Enter here the full names that you have narrowed down from all the names in the world. Describe what you particularly like and dislike about each one of your semi-final favorites.

AND DON'T OVERLOOK...

There are a few things to think about that may seem obvious but are sometimes overlooked in parents' enthusiasm for a particular name. Make sure that the names you are contemplating make a harmonious whole when spoken together. Are they too similar (Andrew Anderson, Hailey Bailey), or inadvertently humorous (Iona House, Siobhan Schindler)? Is there a good balance of syllables? Hugh Kennedy Stone makes a stronger impression than Hugh James Stone, for example, just as Amanda Kate Bellamy has a more pleasant flow than a mouthful like Amanda Clementine Bellamy. Another caveat is to check carefully for possibly embarrassing initials. In other words, if your last name is West, forget about Chelsea Olivia, and if your names end with Taylor, cross Forrest Austin off your list.

A FAMILY OF NAMES

Even if this is your first child, you should consider whether your favorite names will be compatible with others you might choose for your baby's future siblings. Ideally, your children's names should all feel as if they belong in the same family. In your search for harmonious pairings, try to avoid wildly disparate styles (Grace and Dakota), a pair of androgynous names (Bailey and Jordan—which is the boy and which is the girl?), or names whose sounds are close enough to cause confusion (Taylor and Haley). So here is a place to try out an entire family of children's names.

Twins

If you are expecting multiples, experiment with name pairings here, bearing in mind that you'll most likely be saying the two (or three or four) names together, not once but several times a day.

_____   _____

_____   _____

_____   _____

_____   _____

_____   _____

_____   _____

_____   _____

_____   _____

_____   _____

_____   _____

_____   _____

_____   _____

_____   _____

A Multitude of Names

Not that long ago, twins were dressed in identical clothes and given nearly identical names, like Joan and June, April and May, Andy and Mandy. These days, as psychologists stress the importance of treating multiples as separate and unique individuals, parents tend to look for names that are harmonious in more subtle ways.

Consider pairs of classic names (Charles and Elizabeth, Julia and Claire), two names reflecting the same ethnicity (Conor and Maeve, Enzo and Gabriella), two old-fashioned names (Georgia and Louisa, Barnaby and Justin). Just be sure that the pairing doesn't sound too cutesy, too similar, or too disparate in sound or style. With twins it's also important to have clearly defined gender distinctions—boyish or ambisexual names (Morgan and Lane, for instance) can really lead to confusion when your twins are a boy and a girl.

The same guidelines apply if you're expecting more than two. Choosing compatible but distinct names for triplets, quadruplets, or more can be fun and challenging.

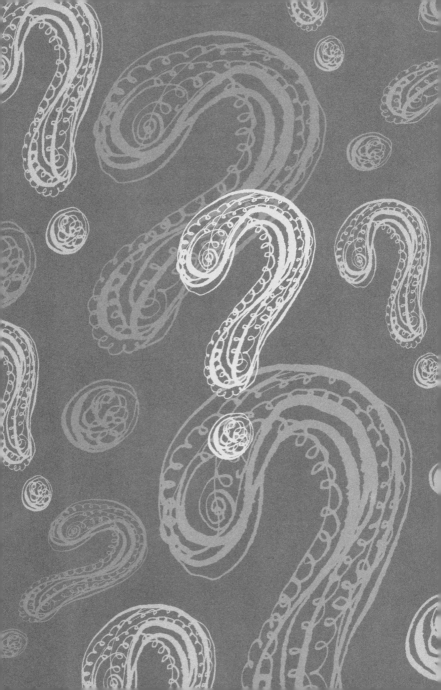

and the name
of the child is

_____

THE CHOSEN NAME

_____

THE MEANING OF THE NAME

_____

_____

WHY WE DECIDED THAT THIS
IS THE PERFECT NAME FOR YOU

_____

_____

DATE AND TIME OF BIRTH